GOD THINGS COME IN SMALL PACKAGES

for Moms

To schedule author appearances, write: Author Appearances, Starburst Promotions, P.O. Box 4123, Lancaster, Pennsylvania 17604 or call (717) 293-0939. Website: www.starburstpublishers.com.

CREDITS:
Cover design by Richmond & Williams
Text design by Steve Diggs and Friends, Nashville

All scripture was taken from the HOLY BIBLE: NEW INTERNATIONAL VERSION® NIV®. Copyright© 1973, 1978, 1984 by International Bible Society.

First Printing, May, 2000
ISBN: 1-892016-29-X
Library of Congress Catalog Number 99–69036
Printed in USA

Contents

INTRODUCTION

By Susan Duke

All that I am or hope to be I owe to my angel mother. I remember my mother's prayers and they have always followed me. They have clung to me all my life. —**Abraham Lincoln**

$\mathcal{A}$ bond exists between mother and child that is powerful beyond belief. It is a bond that spins dreams into the fabric of reality and seats us beside the warm hearth of unconditional love. It is a bond that weaves golden memories—gifts that God gives us to unwrap and enjoy again and again. Gifts of first hugs, fulfilled dreams, healed hurts, life's lessons, and simple everyday pleasures.

God's small packages to mothers are often found wrapped in a giggle, a sigh, a whispered prayer, or a flash of delight. All moms have things in common, but the snippets of life's little celebrations are what makes a mother's experience unique to herself. They are little reminders of a greater gift . . . the gift of calling someone or being called *Mom.*

Motherhood is a noble calling. A calling from God that comes with little "extras." Extra love, extra understanding, and extra perception. God gives to mothers a heart that looks beyond spilled milk, garage-sale jewels, broken jars, and crayon-written notes into a world of wonder . . . a sacred place where time stands still and unveils the gift of a hallowed moment.

We pray each of our stories brings to your life a reminder of the blessings God places in the small, priceless packages of motherhood.

A gift is a precious stone in the eyes of him that hath it: whithersoever it turneth, it prospereth. —Proverbs 17:8

Come to Me when you need a break and I'll give you rest. I'll show you how to live freely and lightly. I satisfy you with good things and renew your youth like the eagle's. I've made the boundaries of your life fall in pleasant places, giving you a delightful inheritance.

Refreshing You,
Your Living God

_____   _____

Matthew 11:28–30; Psalm 103:5; Psalm 16:5

THERE'S NO PLACE
LIKE HOME

By Judy Carden

*E*veryone, it seemed, had plans to leave town for spring break. And with the official start of vacation only hours away, a last-minute getaway seemed unlikely.

"We hate to eat and run," my friend Kathy apologized after she and her family shared a pizza dinner with us, "but we leave for Montana—for the dude ranch—in the morning and we haven't even begun to pack. I'm real sorry your vacation plans fell through. Oh well, there's always next year."

"Yeah . . . next year," I echoed as I shut the front door after them.

Back in the kitchen my three children awaited me.

"What are you doing tomorrow, Mom?" queried Ryan.

"Well now, that depends on who's asking, little buddy," I responded.

"It's me, your favorite six-year-old, silly. And we're taking you somewhere special tomorrow. Meet me in the backyard when *Scooby-Doo* is over. Okay?"

"It's a date."

The following day, at precisely 10 A.M., Danny and Ryan met me in the backyard.

"Where's Aubrey?" I asked.

"Up here—come on up," answered the sweet voice from just above, in our old magnolia tree. "This is your surprise—to spend the day with us in our tree fort."

Moments later, I was nestled in a most unique hideaway. It was a sacred spot of sorts—a place where checkerboard grins ruled the roost. Where a garage-sale plaque declaring "There's No Place Like Home" hung from a rusty nail. Where Oreos were hot and broccoli was not. It was in that secret post, surrounded by magnificent magnolia blossoms, that I learned, firsthand, how friendships were forged, sibling rivalries resolved, and neighborhood dilemmas dissected by the young and the curious.

At afternoon's end, as I gathered a stack of Dr. Seuss books to take back down into the house, Ryan looked at me and asked what I was thinking.

"I was just thinking, little buddy," I said with a wink, "that this is the best vacation a mom could ever have, and that it's true—there really is *no place like home*."

Lord, thank you for turning our restless

hearts back toward home and hearth.

It's so true that, in our search for

happiness, we often forget that the

answer is as close as

our own backyard.

$\mathcal{B}$e sure of what you hope for and certain of what you don't yet see. Childlike faith gains access to My Kingdom. Even the smallest, mustard seed–sized faith has mountain-moving power. May you live by faith and not by sight . . . fixing your eyes on Jesus, the author and perfecter of your faith. Remember, all things are possible with Me.

Faithfully,

Your Promise Keeper

Hebrews 11:1–2; Luke 18:17; Matthew 17:20;
2 Corinthians 5:7; Mark 10:27

UNWAVERING FAITH

By Susan Duke

"Mom! Mom! Come quick!" shouted my ten-year-old son Thomas from the backyard.

I dropped my kitchen dish towel and ran out the backdoor.

Through sobs and sniffles, he explained, "My new bike . . . it's been stolen! It was just here an hour ago and now it's gone!"

I phoned the authorities, but my mother's heart simply wanted to make my son's disappointment and tears go away. A policeman soon arrived at our door. After writing his report, his comments diminished all hopes of finding Thomas' bike. "We've had a rash of bicycle thefts in this area recently. Unfortunately, the likelihood of ever finding that bike is almost zero. Once the thieves disassemble the bikes and sell the parts, it's impossible to track them down."

When he left, I tried to make Thomas understand that he'd probably never see his bike again. "We'll find you another bike soon. I promise."

Thomas' response shocked me. "No, Mom! I don't want another bike. I want *that* bike. It belongs to me, and I'm going to pray that I'll find it."

7

"I understand, Sweetie, but what the policeman said is true."

"I don't care if it's true," Thomas replied emphatically. "You've always told me to have faith when I prayed. God will hear my prayers and I *will* get my bike back. You'll see!"

Oh dear, I thought to myself. *There's nothing I can say without crushing his hopes and determined faith.*

Surprisingly enough, for two days, Thomas remained cheerful and optimistic. Anytime I tried evaluating the situation, hinting at the inevitable outcome, he scolded me for my lack of faith.

On the third day after the theft, I was cooking dinner, when the front door flew open and Thomas came running and leaping into the house. "Mom! Mom! Come quick! I found my bike three streets away from here! God answered my prayers!"

Tears flooded my heart and cheeks as I grabbed my son and held him close, sharing his joy and reward of faith.

Sometimes our grown-up logic is a stumbling block to having childlike faith. Thomas' faith rekindled in me a fresh fire of faith that remains today and confidently reminds me that "nothing is impossible to him who believes."

Someone once penned, "Faith is not

belief without proof, but trust without

reservation." Children are great

teachers when it comes to trusting.

They teach us the simplicity of true

prayer and unwavering faith.

*T*here is a time for everything! It's hard to let go, but the day may come when your child will leave you, to be united in marriage. Don't worry, just as you tenderly comfort your child, I will comfort you. I bottle each precious tear you cry. My compassions for you never fail and are new every morning.

Faithfully,
Your God of All Comfort

Ecclesiastes 3:11; Genesis 2:24; Isaiah 66:13;
Psalm 56:8; Lamentations 3:22–23

THE HANDKERCHIEF

By Caron Loveless

$\mathcal{I}$ expected a little emotion. What mother isn't weepy at the wedding of her firstborn son? But this was getting ridiculous. I cried putting makeup on, wept getting my hair done, and sobbed all the way down the interstate. Weddings are supposed to be joyous occasions and this, of all weddings, was one I was truly happy about!

Before the ceremony I plucked lint from Josh's jacket and groped for profound last words. I smoothed his hair, patted his back, and waited in anguish for our last official walk together. I told myself, *Get a grip. No one's dying here.* But my heart wasn't fooled. A glorious season had ended. Our family would forever be changed and the reality of this was rough.

Finally Josh turned and said, "This is it, Mom." I wiped the wet trails off my cheeks, eked out a smile, and locked my arm into his.

11

In a moment we had reached my seat and, dread of all dreads, our last hug good-bye. I wrapped my arms around him and whispered, "I love you so much." But he was already gone and with a strange, glazed look he gently untangled my arms from his neck and took his place at the front of the church.

That's when I saw it. Lying there in my chair was a crisp, white handkerchief with my initials embroidered on it. It had come from Rebecca, Josh's beautiful bride. Months earlier, while in Africa, she had seen this handkerchief and bought it for me in anticipation of this moment. And as I wiped the tears from my eyes I felt both God and Rebecca saying, "I know this is the hardest thing you've ever done. It's a day of celebration, but it's also all right to cry. Your tears are the purest evidence of a loving mother's heart."

As women, our emotions run high and deep, far and

wide, and they are never more stretched and tested than

in situations regarding our children. Thank God for

your womanly wiring—it's a gift he's entrusted to you.

And allow your most sensitive days to dig sparkling

wells in your soul.

*R*emember and celebrate *this* day I've made. Even before you were born, I personally ordained each and every day of your life. I know the plans I have for you and your family. I have plans to prosper you and not to harm you. When you love Me and are called according to My purposes, you'll have a hope-filled future because I'll cause everything (even heartache) to work together for your good.

Celebrating You,

Your God of Love

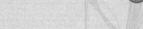

Psalm 118:24; Psalm 139:16; Jeremiah 29:11; Romans 8:28

HEART DAY CELEBRATION

By LeAnn Weiss

$\mathcal{M}$y siblings, five-year-old Steve and three-year-old Sharon pressed their little noses against the window, trying to see what our new prospective mom looked like as my dad pulled the car into the driveway of our parsonage. When I was six, my mommy, JoAnn, had been killed in a car accident, leaving Dad to raise the four of us. Today, Dad was bringing Sandy home to meet us for the first time.

Sharon ran to the door to greet them. Dad was so excited that he forgot my little sister's name. My brother Steve turned shy and ran to hide under an end table. Dressed in slacks, Sandy got down on all fours and crawled over to meet Steve on his level.

Later, she gave us each small gifts: sticker books for the two youngest and scrapbooks for my older sister Pat and me. Sharon must have sensed wedding bells. When Sandy slipped out of the room for a few minutes, Sharon probed, "Where is she? Where did she go? Mama!" Later we learned they had become engaged the previous night.

Sandy officially became our mom on March 24, 1973. Several years later, Mom asked God for wisdom to show her something special she could do to demonstrate how much she valued us. She would never be able to tell us about our births, but the idea came of celebrating that January 26, 1973, the day we first met.

Every celebration needs a cake, Mom thought as she began preparations. Realizing that four active children would devour one cake in no time, she baked separate cakes for each of us, wanting us to savor the event. After decorating the cakes and the room for the party, Mom gathered the four of us around the kitchen table. Our eyes danced as each of us found our own heart-shaped cake waiting to be eaten. Each cake was frosted with a different color so we could tell which one was ours. Amidst the excitement, one of us cheered, "Hey, it's Heart Day!"

The name "Heart Day" stuck. Mom started a tradition of celebrating and giving us gifts each January 26. As the years went by and we grew older, we in turn began sending Mom heart-shaped gifts each Heart Day in remembrance of that day God united our hearts.

In his great plan, God has a way of

assigning special mothers to

children. He knits hearts together,

binding them with his love each day

and forever.

My joy is your strength. I bestow glory on you, lifting up your head. Through faith in My Son, you can come to Me with freedom and confidence. My precepts are right, bringing joy to your heart. My commands are radiant, giving light to your eyes. Watch Me supply and increase your store of seed and enlarge the harvest of your righteousness.

Joyfully,
Your God Most High

——————————— ———————————

Nehemiah 8:10; Psalm 3:3; Ephesians 3:12; Psalm 19:8; 2 Corinthians 9:10

PLANTING SUNFLOWER
DREAMS

By Susan Duke

$\mathcal{W}$hile driving the two hours to help host her long-awaited housewarming party, the anticipation of seeing my grown-up daughter's first real home brought tears to my eyes. I reflected on memories of watching my little girl dress up, play house, and make believe she was a wife and mommy. But today was real.

My eyes danced with delight as I drove into the driveway. The serene country ambience was everything Kelly had described and the perfect setting for she and Robert to raise eight-year-old Kara. When she first called me with her news, I asked if she'd thought of a name for her very own little corner of the world. We tossed around a few names that might fit and finally decided on *Sunflower Meadows*.

I grabbed the mixed sunflower bouquet from the backseat and walked to the front door. "Hello! I'm here!" I called out as I let myself in. The entryway and living room looked like a life-size dollhouse! And my not-so-little girl was busily preparing refreshments in the spacious farmhouse-style kitchen.

19

As I walked through the kitchen door, I was taken aback by the homey blue-and-white checked wallpaper and the décor of countless sunflowers! It was charming and inviting. "Oh, Honey! This is wonderful! And look at what you've done with this kitchen—it's absolutely breathtaking." Kelly loved sunflowers, but I'd never realized how much. "You know, I don't think I've ever asked, but just *why do you love sunflowers so much*?"

"Because, Mom, if I could be a flower, a sunflower is what I'd be."

"But why?" I asked curiously.

"Sunflowers are strong," Kelly explained. "No matter where you plant them, their bright, happy faces always turn toward the sun. And to me, that has special meaning. I too want to always follow *the* SON."

A double blessing sprouts inside a mom's heart when her dreams and her children's dreams come true. My heart smiled as I realized that the most important seed of all I'd planted years ago for my daughter was blooming right before my eyes.

A child's heart is fertile soil for

planting a garden of dreams. Moms

are God's gardeners and not only have

the privilege of nurturing and tending

dreams, but reap a harvest of joy

when they are fulfilled.

*R*emember, the secret things belong to Me. The things I reveal to you belong to you and your children forever. I make known to you the path of life, offering you the recipe for abundant life. In Me you live and move and experience the richness of life. How great is the love that I've lavished upon you, calling you My own child.

Loving You,
Your Abba Father

———————————— ⊙ ————————————

Deuteronomy 29:29; Psalm 16:11; John 10:10;
Acts 17:28; 1 John 3:1

A COOKIE LOVER'S SECRET

By Judy Carden

*I*t was definitely the "come on, Mom, you never have time for us anymore" that propelled me to the kitchen. Consequently, within a matter of minutes, my children and I were shoulder to shoulder—baking a batch of chocolate chip cookies.

As we began our familiar routine of folding, chopping, and mixing the ingredients, Aubrey performed a cheerleading chant. The words on her lime green T-shirt described her mood: "To shout is human, to cheer is divine."

Danny informed us about the new kid on the block, and Ryan entertained us with tales of his fourth-grade classroom.

As I pulled the last tray from the oven, their dad backed his Blazer into the driveway. Lured through the garage by the scent of chocolate chip cookies, he flashed a toothy grin, saying, "I know what y'all are baking." And then, with rapt attention, we listened while he shared the events of his day.

Glancing around at my family, I smiled. Milk mustaches and chocolate smudges encircled their mouths. "Mom," inquired Aubrey, "just what *is* the most important part of your secret recipe?"

"The truth is," I replied with a shrug, "I'm not really sure."

Moments later, in the aftermath of our feast, unmatched plastic glasses line the kitchen counter. An empty milk jug teeters on top of the trash bag. Traces of cookie crumbs remain underneath the cooling racks. And next to the racks, the recipe card. At the bottom of the card is the faded notation: "For best results take no shortcuts." I smile as I realize I've found the secret ingredient after all.

Within two hours, any evidence of our great cookie caper would vanish except for the lingering aroma of semi-sweet morsels.

As I think back to the echoes of appreciation from my family ("Thanks Mom—we're going to remember these times forever and ever"), I pray I will always remember the secret ingredient in the recipe of motherhood: Savor the little moments—and for best results, take no shortcuts.

God gives mothers all the ingredients

necessary to mix abundant batches of

love—where every moment is a

memory in the making.

$\mathcal{I}$'ve made you rich in every way so that you can demonstrate a lifestyle of generosity. Discover that it *truly* is more blessed to give than it is to receive. Cheerful givers win My heart. When you are generous, I'll prosper your life. When you refresh others, you'll be refreshed. I've given you My Spirit as a deposit, guaranteeing what I have awaiting you.

Generously,
Your God

——————————— · ———————————

2 Corinthians 9:7, 11; Acts 20:35; Proverbs 11:25;
2 Corinthians 5:5

YOU NEVER KNOW WHAT YOU'RE GOING TO FIND

By Caron Loveless

$\mathcal{I}$t was a Saturday morning and the kids had awakened to wonderful news. The neighbors were having a garage sale. To my boys a garage sale was almost like winning the lottery because, according to one son, "You never know what cool stuff you're going to find."

"Mom, I gotta go!" yelled Josh, my eight-year-old. "Willy has some really great stuff over there and it's going fast!"

"All right," I called, "but don't spend your savings money!"

"I know!"

It was easy to imagine the really great stuff at Willy's garage sale because we already had some not-so-mint-condition baseball cards, worn-out video games, and a Puerto Rican soccer shirt from his last one. But I didn't mind. I got garage-sale fever myself sometimes and, besides, I was training future husbands in the finer points of bargain hunting.

An hour or so later Josh returned.

"Well, did you get all that great stuff you were after?" I asked.

"Well, yes and no. I decided not to buy anything for me this time. But, close your eyes . . . I got something for you."

Then in my outstretched palm he placed a cool, metal object and when I opened my eyes I saw a slightly tarnished costume-jewelry pin. I wasn't exactly sure, but it looked like a basket with pastel-colored eggs in it.

"Oh, Josh," I said, misty-eyed, "it's just beautiful! What made you decide to do this?"

"Well, I just saw it and thought you might like it. Willy's mom was selling it for a really good price."

"Oh, Honey. I don't know, but this may be the finest gift you've ever given me."

"Do you really like it?"

"Do I like it? Do I like it!" I said, squeezing him hard. "You watch. Tomorrow morning I'll show you just how much I like it."

And the next day, as Josh sat beaming up at me, I walked out to lead the worship at our church wearing the most priceless piece of jewelry I'd ever owned.

It is not the price of the present but the heart of the giver

that lingers the longest in our memory. God loves a

cheerful giver. So live to give with a jubilant heart and

your children will never forget you.

Y ou and your children are My workmanship, created in Christ Jesus to do good works which I've already prepared in advance for you to do. When you train your children in the way they should go, they'll continue following your example when they are old. Blessings as you spur your children on toward love and good deeds.

Creatively,

Maker of All Things

_____   _____

Ephesians 2:10; Proverbs 22:6; Hebrews 10:24

A LITTLE ENCOURAGEMENT
WENT A LONG WAY

By LeAnn Weiss

$\mathcal{G}$rowing up, we always enjoyed reading the home-made smiley-face cards my mom often tucked in our school sack lunches. Each card contained a short magic-marker-written message, like, "LeAnn, Remember I love you and am thinking happy thoughts of you! Hugs & Kisses, Mom."

Mom made all of our cards, not just for birthdays, but for every occasion. We sometimes found her cards, which usually contained Bible verses, taped to our bathroom mirror and throughout our house. It was a treat to discover Mom's heart-shaped construction-paper love notes on our pillows. She even included corny get well cards alongside our bowls of chicken soup when we were sick. When Mom observed us doing something good, we often received one of her "I'm proud of you" cards, complimenting what we had done. She frequently surprised us with her custom-tailored messages of love, encouragement, appreciation, correction, and challenge. As we grew older, Mom taught us how to make our own cards. Some family nights we had fun creating cards and stationery together.

It wasn't until years later that we discovered how Mom's home-made card tradition originated. Before Mom married my widowed dad, she had lived comfortably on her salary as an educational director and enjoyed buying fine cards and gifts. But as a newlywed instant mom, she found that Hallmark cards weren't an option anymore. My dad's budget didn't allow for many extras, especially since he was already raising four (and later five) children on a pastor's salary. Consequently, Mom started making her own cards, incorporating the creativity she had developed during her earlier days teaching kindergarten. And so the tradition began.

As an adult I continued the tradition, making my own cards for family and friends. Eventually in 1994, after promptings from many who had received my personalized cards and Scripture gifts, I started Encouragement Company. God orchestrated a series of events two years later and I began writing paraphrased scriptures for the now popular Hugs series. Little did Mom realize, during all those years she crafted our cards with love, that her encouragement would go such a long way.

Remember . . . little eyes are watching

you. Even the small things you do as a

mom can have a profound impact on

the destiny of your children long after

they've left your nest.

$\mathcal{M}$y understanding of your circumstances has no limits. I will not leave you comfortless. Instead, I'll come to you, personally comforting you. I am so good to you! My love for you never runs out. My faithfulness continues to your children, and your children's children, forever . . . through all generations.

Love Always,
Your Good God

——————————— ———————————

Psalm 147:5; John 14:18; Isaiah 51:12; Psalm 100:5

THE COMFORTER

By Judy Carden

$\mathcal{I}$ waved vigorously until the white Blazer carrying my husband and our nineteen-year-old daughter was out of sight.

"I love you, Tallahassee Lassie! God bless you!" I yelled down the empty emerald-arched, tree-lined street. Only the squirrels were stirring as I shuffled back into the house.

The last few days had been a flurry of activity as our family helped Aubrey prepare for her return to Florida State University in Tallahassee. And now, she was on her way. Without a thought, I went into her room and sat down on her daybed. My eyes scanned the room to find something, anything, that might comfort me after sending my precious college coed back into her academic world.

Yet my search was in vain, for the only hint of familiarity were the yellow walls that, until this morning, held her favorite posters.

I could feel the onset of a solo pity party. I grabbed the comforter at the end of the bed and pulled it tightly around me. Clinging to the comforter, I was also clinging to the hope that Aubrey was taking the one thing that mattered most back to college with her—God.

Although I hadn't pressed her lately about her relationship with God, I remember that during the summer, she often mistook my own exuberance as an "I'm checking on you and your faith" attitude.

"Mom, I need some space," she would gently remind me. But this morning I felt grieved wondering if, while she crammed her worldly possessions into the Blazer, she tucked God's love and promise somewhere in between her army-green clothing trunk and Granddaddy's old microwave.

As I tugged on a corner of the comforter, a yellow Post-it Note fell from the soft cotton fold and fluttered to the floor. Bending down to retrieve it, I immediately recognized Aubrey's handwriting.

"GOD IS SO GOOD TO ME!!" The bold-lettered message read.

I smiled as I clutched the message to my chest, realizing that God cared enough to reassure and comfort me through a note that would be forever posted on the door of my heart.

And as I left Aubrey's room, I whispered, "He's good to me, too, my Tallahassee Lassie—He's good to me, too."

Trusting our children to the Lord is

sometimes one of the hardest things to

do. And yet, when we do, he is faithful

to confirm our dedication

of their care to him.

$\mathcal{N}$ever fear because I'm your light and your salvation. I watch over all who love Me. I haven't given you a spirit of fear. Instead, I've empowered you with boldness, love, and self-discipline. I've made My light shine in your heart to give you knowledge of My Glory. You can sleep in peace for I alone make you dwell in safety.

Peacefully,
Your God of Light

———————   ◦   ———————

Psalm 27:1; Psalm 145:20; 2 Timothy 1:7;
2 Corinthians 4:6; Psalm 4:8

LET THERE BE LIGHT

By Susan Duke

"Do you think bears live in these woods?" asked six-year-old Tyler.

"Well, they just might," his grandfather answered.

"Have you ever seen one?" chimed four-year-old Rachel.

"No, but I may have heard one growl once," her grandfather humored her.

Tyler's deep brown eyes twinkled as he continued his query about the woodland creatures occupying the dense woods surrounding our log home.

Brenda, my stepdaughter, tucked the kids in bed for the night after a long day of catching grasshoppers in a jar, enjoying a hearty country supper, and taking bubble baths. Afterwards, she joined us in the living room, but soon noticed the bedroom light was on again.

She heaved a tired sigh as she trudged back down to turn the light off once more. She'd just returned and plopped on the sofa when the light clicked on again. We heard Tyler and Rachel chattering away.

"Let me see what I can do," I offered, sensing Brenda's exasperation.

Reaching their room, I turned out the light, sat on the edge of the bed, and asked, "Don't you know if your mom has to come in here one more time, you're going to really be in trouble?"

"But we don't want the light off!" whined Rachel.

"Do you sleep with it on at home?" I asked.

"No."

"Then why do you want it on here?"

"'Cause we're scared," Tyler offered.

"Scared of what? You're safe here!"

"Well, do the bears ever come up to the house at night?" asked Tyler.

"Of course not! Your granddad was just kidding you! There are no bears out here! You never have to be afraid. Besides, Jesus lives in your heart, so even in the dark, there's a light shining there all the time." I kissed them goodnight and turned off the light.

Ten minutes passed when, once more, filtered light came shining down the hallway. I bounded toward the bedroom, disappointed they would take our words so lightly.

"What's the deal, kids?"

"Well . . . we know Jesus is in here," Tyler explained. "And we know he's not scared. But he also talks to you in your heart and he just said he'd rather sleep with the light on."

Even adults experience fear at times, but God's light is

always on, shining brightly to dispel the darkness and

replace the shadows of fear with a beacon of faith.

$\mathcal{R}$emember . . . I've accepted you. My thoughts of you are so precious. It doesn't matter who is against you because I am for you! Charm is deceptive and beauty is fleeting, but a woman who fears Me is to be praised. Outwardly, you're growing older, but inwardly I'm renewing you with each day. You can be confident that I will faithfully complete the good work I've started in you.

Thinking Good
Thoughts of You,

Your Almighty God

———————— ⊛ ————————

Romans 15:7; Romans 8:31; Psalm 139:17;
Proverbs 31:30; 2 Corinthians 4:16; Philippians 1:6

THE NOTE

By Caron Loveless

$\mathcal{I}$ thought I'd been handling the aging process pretty well until one evening when I was riding my bike down the sidewalk.

Next to me was a busy street, and a car drove by with some teenage boys in it. Music blared out their rolled-down windows and as they passed me a boy in the front leaned out and shouted some pointedly unkind remarks. *The nerve of that guy!* I thought, peddling faster.

A few minutes later a different car passed and the same thing happened again! So then I thought, *Okay, I know I'm not getting any younger, but I'm not as bad as all that, certainly not worth this drive-by series of "off-color" commentaries.*

But, naturally, I went home feeling just a touch dejected and a little insecure—how else would a middle-aged mom feel after such an experience?

That night, my husband was out of town so I recounted the incidents to my teenage sons and asked them what they thought.

Joseph said, "I'm really sorry, Mom, but you know how kids are." And Jon, my quiet one, the boy who thinks "yeah," "nope," and "I dunno" are all the words a man needs in life, looked up and said, "I hope you got their license tag number because I'd like to pay them a little visit."

I laughed and thought that was the end of it until later that evening when I got in bed and reached out to turn off the light. A piece of notebook paper with the word "Mom" was taped to the lampshade, and it read: "Mom, What you told me about those guys really disturbed me. I have the coolest mom this side of the Mississippi. Don't let anyone else tell you that you don't look good. I believe you're the best, so nothing else should matter! Love, Jon."

For a long time I just held the note and smiled. Then I turned out the light and lay in the dark, thanking God for his timely encouragement and the sweet, sensitive son he prompted to deliver it.

God calls us the apples of his eye,

the jewels in his crown, his chosen,

beloved children, and his bride.

Focus on these things. For,

ultimately, it's how God sees us, not

how we see ourselves, that

strengthens our personal

confidence.

*W*hatever your hand finds to do, do it right with all your might. Let Me give you a spirit of unity among yourselves as you follow Jesus, so that you will glorify Me together. Even a child is known by his actions. Whatever you do, put your whole heart into it, giving your very best, as if you're doing it for Me. I'll reward you.

Cheering You On,
Your Heavenly Coach

Ecclesiastes 9:10; Romans 15:5–6; Proverbs 20:11; Colossians 3:23–24

A TEAM OF MY OWN

By Judy Carden

$\mathcal{F}$amilies have different approaches to child rearing. Some leave each to their own devices, while others foster competition among members. Still others use a team approach to build unity—with each child working to help the others succeed. A few years back I experienced the team approach—though, left to my own devices, I might have chosen a different route.

When I agreed to an intense, three-week writing project, I thought it best to hire a temporary housekeeper to take over my chores.

"We can help you," insisted my children, then ages fifteen, thirteen, and ten. Their reaction caught me completely off guard, since they were not task oriented in the least. Though I desperately wanted the housekeeper, I felt I owed them the chance to fail.

On the Saturday before my deadline, I heard an unusual sound from the guest bathroom. Moments later, I found Danny, radio headset covering his ears, toilet brush in hand, vigorously swirling the insides of the toilet bowl and yelling, "Go! Run! Touchdown! Touchdown!" (I learned there is a direct correlation between a running back scoring and the speed with which a toilet can be cleaned.)

Aubrey was chief cook and bottle washer. And though not everything she cooked could be identified, the guys never failed to compliment her on her creativity.

And while it was true that the boys' room did not meet with my normal standard of cleanliness—even the roaches and ants evacuated at one point—I simply shut the door.

All things considered, it was a productive three weeks. For, in addition to meeting my deadline, I realized that if moms don't challenge their families' sense of unity and commitment, children will never identify what it is to be part of a team. Because the family is our first team experience, these training years are irreplaceable.

And though I was less than warm to the initial plan, and silently doubted its prospect for success while in progress, there is one thing I would still like to say to my children: I sure am glad we're on the same team.

Lord, thank you for the many

teachable moments of motherhood

where milestones are measured by

the heart of the family.

$y$ou are My holy and chosen treasured possession. I am able to protect all that you entrust to Me until that day. Avoid unwholesome words. Only speak words that will help build others up according to their needs. Remember, I've given you this treasure in jars of clay to show that this all-surpassing power is from Me and not from you.

Cherishing You,
Your God of Glory

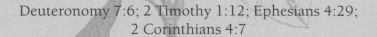

Deuteronomy 7:6; 2 Timothy 1:12; Ephesians 4:29;
2 Corinthians 4:7

TREASURED POSSESSIONS

By Susan Duke

"Judy, whatever happened to that huge antique pickle jar you used to have? You know, the one you always filled with your famous popcorn recipe?" I asked.

"Oh, Suzie, there's a story about what happened to that jar," Judy replied in hushed tones.

Every Thanksgiving and Christmas, Judy created a special recipe of popcorn, butter, white syrup, and pecans. One bite and you were hooked! No one has ever been able to eat just one of the tasty chunks that easily pulls apart from the delicious mixed concoction. So . . . she always made a huge batch and stored it in her most treasured possession—a large, old pickle jar she'd had for years. The unique glass container and its delectable contents became part of our family tradition and every special gathering was filled with the anticipated arrival of Judy's famous popcorn jar.

We were packing to leave for a second Thanksgiving celebration out of town. I asked my daughter Amanda to put the jar in the backseat of the car. I looked up just in time to see the jar bump the side of the car, crash to the ground, and shatter into thousands of tiny pieces. My heart sank and I shouted, "Amanda, you never pay attention to what you're doing! Don't you know that was my most prized possession?"

"But, Suzie," Judy continued, "when Amanda looked up and I saw her little ashen face, God quickened something in me that I'll never forget: *Broken jars can be replaced, but little broken hearts can't.* Amanda's shattered heart was much more important than that old shattered jar . . . and I knew that I was looking at my most treasured possession—my precious daughter.

"Immediately I called to Amanda, 'Baby, I'm so sorry I said that. That old jar is not important and it's *not* my most prized possession. You are!'"

God's message was clear. It's our relationships that are important, not our possessions. So often we place too much value on things. And as moms, we've been given the greatest irreplaceable treasure God could possibly give: our children.

Relationships are the greatest

blessings in our lives. As moms, we

should never miss an opportunity to

instill this simple truth into our

children and impart to them that they

are truly a treasure and the most

valuable gift God has given us.

I created your inmost being and knitted you together in your mother's womb. I've made you fearfully and wonderfully, fashioning you in My own image. You're a reflection of My glory. Remember, you're being transformed into My likeness with an ever-increasing glory radiating My Spirit.

Love,
Your Creator and
Heavenly Father

Psalm 139:13–14; Genesis 1:27; 2 Corinthians 3:18

EMILY'S GIFT

By Caron Loveless

$\mathcal{L}$auri was a month old when she was adopted by two very warm and affectionate parents. Instantly she was a cherished child and her mother and father gave her all the love and devotion any daughter could want.

But there was one thing Lauri's parents could not give her: their likeness.

Lauri had sunny blonde hair, blue eyes, and creamy white skin and looked drastically different from her parents, aunts, uncles, and cousins, whose hair, eyes, and complexions were all much darker. And as Lauri grew up this distinction began to trouble her.

Whenever Lauri was introduced, people would say, "Well where did this child come from? She looks nothing like the rest of you." On trips to the beach, Lauri's older sister, also adopted, was free to play in the sun for hours because even she had dark hair and olive skin. But fair-haired Lauri was made to sit in the car and read books so she wouldn't get sunburned. Worse than that, one set of Lauri's grandparents never fully received her as their own.

Until she delivered her firstborn child.

Childbirth is an overwhelming experience for every mother, but for Lauri one extra emotional element was added in. There, snuggled against her chest, lay Emily, a perfect little blonde-haired, blue-eyed, fair-skinned copy of herself.

"Look at her!" Lauri cried to her husband, eyes glistening, "I never realized how much it mattered . . . Oh, Scott, she looks just like me!"

Lauri had never resembled anyone before and for the very first time in her life felt the relational connection she'd always missed.

Now when Lauri braids Emily's hair or gazes into her eyes there's a bond like she's never known. She rests, comforted in the truth that her Heavenly Father sees even the innermost longings of her heart and her blonde-haired, blue-eyed daughter is living proof.

We were made in the image of God and we belong to

him. Because we are his, the family resemblance is

unmistakable. But God's greatest joy comes

as our hearts and our habits mirror his.

$\mathcal{L}$et your heart weigh your responses to life's challenges. Laughter is good medicine for the stresses of motherhood. Don't miss out on the continual feast of a happy heart.

Smiling on You,
Your God of Joy

———————— ⬤ ————————

Proverbs 15:28; Proverbs 17:22; Proverbs 15:13, 15

.

A JIGGLING BOX OF JOY

By LeAnn Weiss

*W*hen Barbara returned from shopping, she knew immediately by the laughter and commotion in the kitchen that her sons were up to something. But walking into the kitchen, she couldn't believe her eyes. Her four boys, ages sixteen to eight, were sitting at the table using spoons to fling the raspberry Jell-O with banana chunks, which she had made earlier that day, at her formerly spotless white brick kitchen wall. It was obvious that her oldest son, Tim, who was supposed to maintain order while she was gone, was the ringleader.

The shrieks of exhilaration and accompanying sound effects from the flying red missiles hitting the wall came to an abrupt halt when the boys realized their mother's presence. The silence was deafening as they awaited their sentence. Each of them mentally prepared their last wills and testaments as their mom stood shaking her head in disbelief. They knew that this caper was going to test even *her* sense of humor.

As Barbara stared first at the wall and then at the boys, they just knew she was debating whether to scream, faint, spank, ground them for life, or kill them. They were caught red-handed.

But realizing that the kids were going to have to clean up the mess anyway, Barbara finally responded, "Where's *my* spoon?"

Shocked but relieved that his mother was joining their escapade, Tim handed her the biggest cooking ladle he could find. After watching their mom send several ladles full of Jell-O and bananas beaming at the wall, the boys breathed a collective sigh of relief. Then for the next fifteen minutes, the five of them slung red globs of Jell-O together, laughing hysterically all the while. By the time they ran out of ammunition, the entire wall was a sticky red mess.

Of course, Barbara supervised as her boys spent the next two hours scrubbing down the wall and kitchen floor. More than thirty years later, Barbara still chuckles that God gave her the foresight to transform the raspberry caper into a memory the Johnsons will never forget. They still laugh each time they see Jell-O commercials, having experienced the true fun found inside that small box.

A God-sized perspective mixed with

a good sense of humor goes a long

way in helping moms to enjoy

their children and create

lasting memories.

$\mathcal{I}$'ve already given you everything you need for life and godliness. Learn the life-freeing secret of being content in all circumstances, whether you have plenty or are in want. Godliness with contentment is great gain. Materialism and envy only lead to decay, but when your heart is at peace, you experience life. Don't worry, I'll faithfully supply all of your needs according to My limitless riches in glory.

My All Sufficiency,

Your God and Faithful

Provider

2 Peter 1:3; Philippians 4:12, 19; 1 Timothy 6:6; Proverbs 14:30

A DRAWER FULL OF CONTENTMENT

By Judy Carden

"Mommy, when is the moving van coming?" eight-year-old Aubrey called out to me, her voice echoing throughout our empty house.

"Soon, baby—any day now," I assured her. But the truth was, I couldn't bear to tell her that I didn't know when, or if, we would ever see the possessions that once filled the beautiful home we had left behind.

In the months following our cross-country move, after the children and I gave way to restless slumber, dreams of yesterday would dance in my head. Memories of candlelit dinners, complete with hand-cut crystal, sparkling silver, and freshly cut flowers, seemed so real I could almost reach out and touch it all—and then . . . I'd awaken.

Looking around at my stark surroundings, reality let me in on a little secret: I no longer lived in that lovely home. I was now a widow, a single mom . . . and we were poor. Yes, we had shelter, but for reasons unimportant to this story, the moving van never came.

"Oh, God," I wailed one morning. "Look at us! How can you expect me to be happy in this squalor? We have nothing!" The answer he promptly provided my heart was clear and concise: *Contentment must come from within—no matter what the circumstances.*

And so began my quest for contentment.

Our finest piece of furniture was a thirty-six-inch-high cardboard dresser of drawers. What little clothing we had was stored in boxes from our local supermarket. We ate on the floor, slept on the floor, and wore our knees out praying on those same hard, cold floors.

We built sandcastles by day and watched star-studded light shows by night. We roller skated, finger painted, and played sandlot baseball. And we laughed. A lot.

Eleven years later, though my present home is lovely, the dilapidated dresser remains—as God's reminder that my contentment has little to do with possessions and everything to do with priorities, purpose, and the people I love.

Contentment is the place in our heart

where life's simple pleasures produce

countless treasures.

Sacrifice pleases Me. Don't forget to do good and share with others. Remember, I loved you so much, that I gave My only Son to R.S.V.P a place in heaven for all who believe in Him.

Preparing a Place
for You,
Your Heavenly Father

——————— ⬤ ———————

Hebrews 13:16; John 3:16; John 14:2–3

SPECIAL RESERVATIONS

By Susan Duke

$\mathcal{W}$e awakened—not to sounds of a ringing alarm clock, but to muffled whispers and a succession of gentle rapping on our bedroom door.

"Mom! Dad! Are you awake? We're coming in!"

The door opened and we peered out of half-opened eyelids as two winsome elves, carrying a red wicker tray and jingling bells, made their way to our bedside. The tray was brimming with a scrumptious breakfast feast of scrambled eggs, heart-shaped toast, bacon, hot steaming coffee, and orange juice.

"Merry Christmas . . . early," eleven-year-old Thomas said, grinning mischievously.

"We have a surprise for you!" Kelly (then fourteen years old) chimed in.

"This *is* a surprise! I said, while clumsily fluffing pillows behind my back.

"There's more," Kelly explained as she handed us a big, colorful, handwritten card.

Their eyes twinkled as we unfolded the paper and read the words, "YOU ARE INVITED—to a night on the town at the Magic Time Machine. Reservations already made!"

The Magic Time Machine was a fun, upbeat, but very expensive, restaurant reputable for its wonderful food and atmosphere. We were perplexed as to how these two angels of good will could pull off such an extravagant feat.

"How can you afford this?" my husband asked.

"Don't worry. Everything's covered. This is our Christmas gift to you and Mom," Kelly assured.

From the moment we entered the restaurant, our waiter, dressed as Felix the Cat, helped us enjoy a wonderfully fun evening of festive celebration.

"Just give me the bill," Thomas quipped smugly to the waiter at the end of the night.

Not only was the waiter shocked that a kid was paying the exorbitant tab, but he was pleasantly surprised when Thomas left a bigger tip than any he'd ever likely received.

Later that night Kelly and Thomas confessed they'd secretly earned eighty dollars by raking neighbors' leaves and sweeping sidewalks. They figured that would be enough.

It was enough.

Enough . . . knowing our children's sacrifice of love far exceeded any invitation we'd ever again receive in this lifetime. But also enough . . . to remind us of another Christmas many years ago; and another invitation to a feast in a great place called Heaven.

And enough to know . . . that reservations have already been made.

As parents we think of ourselves as

the ones who give to our children. But

so often, it is the gifts they plan, work

for, and creatively present to us that

invite us into the sanctuary of their

souls, where we are given a sacred

glimpse at eternity.

*W*hen you call upon Me, I'll answer you. I don't despise you when you're wounded or suffering. I listen to your cry for help and am your ever-present help in trouble. When you love Me and are called according to My higher purposes, I even turn the disappointments and hurts of your life into unexpected showers of blessings.

Reliably,

Your Redeemer

Psalm 86:7; Psalm 22:24; Psalm 46:1; Romans 8:28

BAND-AIDS AND
BLESSINGS

By Caron Loveless

$\mathcal{I}$t was prime time at the grocery store when Joann and her young daughter Judith got their turn in the crowded checkout line.

As usual, Judith was a ready helper, pulling her favorite foods out of the cart almost as fast as the cashier could scan them. But when Joann began tossing items onto the belt she suddenly scratched her hand on the basket. "Doggone!" she said. "I keep reopening that old cut. Oh, Judith, I meant to get more Band-Aids."

With her hand freely bleeding, Joann looked around for a tissue until Judith stopped her. She reached up, took her mother's hand, and then in a very loud voice prayed, "Dear Jesus . . ." At the sound of this, everyone turned toward Judith and stared. But she continued on with confidence, ". . . my mom hurt her hand. Please make her feel better. I know you can do this because you promised you would. Thank you. Your friend, Judith."

The lines on both sides stopped cold. Everyone was nodding or smiling or crying. Then some came by to touch Judith's cheek. Some patted her head or squeezed her hand. Nearly everyone acknowledged this holy moment in the grocery store, which was made even more wonderful by the fact that Judith is a darling little girl with Down's syndrome. Judith may not know a lot of things. But it's clear that in one strategic area she is smarter than most: no matter where she is, if there's trouble, she knows exactly whom to call.

And her mother has not forgotten this. The other day when she went looking for the Band-Aids, she was reminded again of Judith's spontaneous grocery store prayer. It made her smile and whisper a prayer of her own.

Hurts were not meant to be handled alone and wounds

unattended will weaken you. Call on the Lord wherever

you are. Heave all your heartaches to heaven.

$\mathcal{R}$emember, sons are My heritage and your children are gifts of blessing from Me to you. When you welcome a child, you're welcoming Me. If you love one another, I live in you and My love is made complete in you.

Blessing You,
Your God of Every
Good and Perfect Gift

Psalm 127:3; Matthew 18:5; 1 John 4:12; James 1:17

DIAMONDS AND DUMP TRUCKS

By Judy Carden

$\mathcal{I}$t seemed as though Bob and I had just settled in for a short winter's nap when our three little cherubs exploded into our bedroom, bouncing up and down on our bed.

"Santa came! And he finished all of his cookies and milk," Aubrey squealed. "It's Christmas morning!" yelled Danny. "Hurry, hurry," five-year-old Ryan pleaded, bouncing high and landing smack in the middle of his father and me.

Fifteen minutes later, we were positioned around the Christmas tree, waiting to hear the magic words from Dad: "The first gift of Christmas goes to" . . . and, at long last, the festivities were under way.

Soft sounds of Christmas carols and squeals of delight filled the air, as, one by one, the children tore open their gifts.

Then came the moment when all eyes were on me, when Bob handed me a perfectly wrapped, petite box.

"Open it," urged the children.

"Oooohhh," I gasped, as I lifted a brilliant pair of diamond earrings from the box and put them in my ears.

As I glanced around the room, though, I couldn't help but notice that the boys had exchanged worried glances. Danny smacked himself in the forehead and said, "Diamonds. Oh, no."

We continued our celebration until just one gift remained beneath the tree. It was clumsily wrapped, with much too much Scotch tape, and had a tag that read: "To Mom—from your boys."

For the second time that morning all eyes were on me as I ripped away at the layers of paper and tape and ceremoniously lifted their gift for all to see: a set of colorful plastic trucks! Three, to be exact.

"They're for me and you and Danny," Ryan informed me. "But they're not diamonds. Wanna play anyway?"

"They're better than diamonds," I said in between sobs.

And then . . . I removed my earrings, grabbed a yellow dump truck, and said, "Last one to the sandbox is a rotten egg." Because, you know, diamonds are forever . . . but little boys are not.

Heavenly Father, of all gifts

both great and small,

our children are the best of all.

I, even I, am He who comforts you. I command My angels concerning you, to guard you and your family in all of your ways. When you pass through the deep waters and feel like you are drowning, remember I'm with you. I won't let life's fires burn you. My consolation brings joy to your soul. I'll swallow death forever and wipe away all of your tears.

Healing You,
Your God of Sanctuary

———————   ———————

Isaiah 51:12; Psalm 91:11; Isaiah 43:2; Psalm 94:19; Isaiah 25:8

IN THE ARMS OF AN ANGEL

By Susan Duke

*W*hen the phone rang and I heard my friend Charlet's tearful voice, I knew something was wrong. Her daughter-in-law had just miscarried the baby that would have been Charlet's first grandchild. For five months she'd excitedly anticipated the birth of this precious new life.

Charlet was heartbroken. However, as a pastor's wife, she knew she'd have to be strong and attend to responsibilities for the following day's church service.

I normally don't like shopping on Saturdays, but that day, I couldn't get Charlet's grieving voice out of my mind. While loading breakfast dishes into the dishwasher, I tried to think of a special gift that would offer my friend some small comfort and expression of compassion. I thumbed through my mind's index of ideas, but nothing seemed right. As I cleaned my blue tile countertop with my dishtowel, I wiped around a little clay figurine of a chubby-faced angel, holding a baby in its arms.

This little angel had special meaning to me. I keep it in my kitchen, where I spend many hours, away from the angel collection displayed in my living room. My husband Harvey gave me this angel on the first Mother's Day after we lost our son Thomas.

I was reminded that each time Charlet had visited my home, she had admired the angel and its significance. I put down my dish towel, grabbed my purse, and went to a specialty shop to find the exact angel. Later that afternoon, my mission was accomplished. Harvey and I decided we'd attend Charlet's church the next day rather than our own.

We eased into the back row as the worship service began. After the first song, Pastor Ken initiated a time of greeting one another. When Charlet turned and saw me walking toward her, a well of tears filled her eyes. I handed her the gift and said, "Why don't you open this now? I have a feeling you need what's in here today." As she opened the gift, her face emanated a heavenly glow.

"Suzie, you couldn't have known this, but just after I found out we'd lost baby Katherine, I closed my eyes and envisioned an angel holding her. Then immediately I remembered the little angel in your kitchen. I thanked God for showing me she was safely carried to heaven in the arms of an angel."

God's angels are ever near, bringing

messages of comfort and love. Just

when we need a special reminder of

his mercy, God often recruits earthly

vessels to minister his

tender compassion.

$\mathcal{U}$plifting words are as precious as apples of gold in settings of silver! I encourage your heart and strengthen you in every good deed and word. Don't lose heart in doing good in your many duties as mom. For in due time, you're going to see a harvest in the lives of your family if you don't quit. Always remember that you can do all things because I strengthen you.

Love,

Your God of

Encouragement

Proverbs 25:11; 2 Thessalonians 2:17; Galatians 6:9; Philippians 4:13

MILLION-DOLLAR WORDS

By LeAnn Weiss

Shannon was trying to reevaluate some of the decisions she and her husband had made concerning their children. At the end of her first year of teaching Kandee and Tiffany at home, Shannon wanted to make sure continuing with homeschooling was the right choice for her daughters.

All year, Shannon had spent extra time doing special projects to help make learning more fun. Together they made construction-paper animals and wrote stories about each animal. Another time, Shannon bought a large roll of butcher paper that they rolled out over the family room floor. They took turns lying down and tracing each other's bodies. Next, they cut out the life-sized paper dolls, coloring and decorating them to resemble themselves. Shannon followed up with a lesson on how each person is unique and special to God. Sometimes they wrote songs they'd sing together. The girls' eyes sparkled as they cuddled on the couch, listening to their mom read interesting biographies of famous people. Some sunny days, they'd spread out a large blanket in the backyard and hold classes outdoors, observing ants, insects, and other creatures in God's creation. Not to mention the scrumptious picnic lunches they enjoyed. For art, they made sculptures, paintings, and produced plays. Still, Kandee hadn't really expressed whether she enjoyed her mom teaching her or if she missed public school.

Finally, Shannon decided to ask her second grader's opinion. "What do you like about homeschooling?"

"Well, I like your hot lunches and not having to walk to school in the rain," Kandee blurted out. Pausing to think for a moment, she added, "But most of all, I like getting to know you and spending more time with you. You make learning so fun, Mommy." Kandee proceeded to give her mom a big bear hug.

With her daughter's sweet affirmation, all the extra hours of work seemed worth it. Shannon felt like she had just received a million-dollar paycheck in Kandee's words. And she looked forward to the start of the next school year with new anticipation.

Sometimes the confirmation we're

looking for comes from the "mouths of

babes." A mother's priceless reward

for giving time and care comes

wrapped in sweet hugs, smiling faces,

and simple words of love

and appreciation.

*I*t's My good pleasure to reveal My nature to precious children. Because of My great mercy, you've been given birth into living hope through My Son's resurrection from the dead. Remember . . . My Word is a lamp to your child's way and will light your family's paths.

Tenderly,

Your God

P.S. I'll wipe away all of your tears.

———————————— ○ ————————————

Luke 10:21; 1 Peter 1:3; Psalm 119:105; Revelations 21:4

A NOT-SO-ORDINARY
BEDTIME STORY

By Caron Loveless

As Jonathan hopped into the recliner, the sweet smell of soap still clung to him. At four years old he was a tough little boy who'd rather build forts or shoot bad guys than sit still and read with Mom. But somehow I wrestled him down and snuggled him in for a bedtime story.

This time I'd chosen a Bible storybook with bright pictures, short stories, and questions to ask at the bottom of the page. "Can I hold it?" Jonathan asked.

"Uh-huh," I said, putting the book in his lap. "You can turn the pages, too."

And in my best cartoon voice I read while Jonathan listened with unusual attentiveness.

When we came to the story of the crucifixion, there on the page was a picture of Christ on the cross. Jonathan got very still and his face began to change. And as I slowed the pace of my words, out of the corner of my eye I saw tears begin to trickle down his cheek. I paused and tried not to move. This had never happened before. Jonathan was not a crier. He thought tears were illegal, even for little boys.

With my own eyes filling, I reached over and squeezed Jonathan tight and for one holy moment we sat together in silence. Then I said, "You know what, Sweetie? This is not the end of the story. Turn the page and see what happens next."

Quickly we read about the resurrection and talked about heaven. Jonathan relaxed and with eyes glistening he said, "That's better."

I shut the book and he scampered up the ladder to his bunk. Then, tugging the covers to his chin, I kissed the cheek where the teardrops fell and whispered, "Good night, sweet boy."

"Don't close the door all the way," he called after me.

"Okay."

And as I turned out the light, I knew that this had been no ordinary night, that we had shared no ordinary story. God himself had been there, touching my tough boy's heart and using his tears to soften my soul as well.

As we let God tenderize our hearts, we will move more

often to a place of empathy for others. One sign of

compassion is tears, which are so highly prized in heaven

that God himself has kept each one of yours in a bottle.

*R*emember, the prayers of the righteous are powerful and effective. Build yourself up in your most holy faith and prayer. Fight the good fight of faith, taking hold of the eternal life to which you were called when you made your good confession in the presence of many witnesses.

Victoriously,
The Lord, Your Shield

James 5:16; Jude 20; 1 Timothy 6:12

A MAJOR LEAGUE HOME RUN

By Judy Carden

As far as Little League seasons go, it was safe to say eleven-year-old Danny's was a wash—or, at least, that's how his coach saw it, that is. For, no matter what Danny did, the coach criticized him. And while the coach's criticism was meant to be constructive, his temper often got the best of him, turning criticisms into personal attacks.

Once, during pregame warm-ups, coach was reviewing batting technique. All this was lost on Danny, who, after ten minutes, began daydreaming about dragons and dinosaurs.

"Danny!" exploded the coach. "Are you listening?!" he demanded to know with his usual furor. "With the slump you're in, kid, you couldn't hit your way out of a paper bag."

It was true. My son was in a slump, but the coach's unnecessary roughness caused the mother lioness in me to release a mighty roar. I descended from the bleacher planks two by two, eager to defend my son's honor as a player.

As my feet hit the ground, Danny waved me over toward the dugout. "Mom, please don't say anything to coach," he said just loud enough for me to hear. "You can't fix everything." Reluctantly, I returned to my seat as the teams took the field, leaving him to wage his own war.

When the coach again screamed at Danny as he jogged to the batter's box, Danny nonchalantly pointed the tip of his bat downward and, making the sign of the cross in the sand, bowed his head in an obvious moment of prayer. He took a called strike; the next two pitches were high and inside; then, swinging on the fourth pitch, did something he had never done before—he hit a home run.

That would be the only home run he would ever hit before retiring from baseball the following year at the tender age of twelve. But, for Danny, one home run was enough—so much so that on the game ball triumphantly displayed in his bronze holder are the inscribed words: "Moms can't fix everything—but God can."

As mothers, one of the most vital

gifts we can give our children is the

bedrock belief that there is no

greater gain than that which is

granted us through the power

of prayer.

*T*here's no doubt about it . . . you are a woman to be praised! Your value far exceeds that of gems and rubies. You add good to each day. Your life is clothed with strength and dignity. You've contributed many words of wisdom and faithful instruction through the years. Your children arise and call you a blessed mom. Many women do noble things, but *you* surpass them all!

Honoring You,

Your King of Kings

Proverbs 31:10–30

TRIBUTE TO A LIFE
WELL LIVED

By Susan Duke

$\mathcal{T}$he latest saga of my mother's life could be called *More Than One Life to Live*. During her year as a widow at age seventy-seven, I found myself in the reversed role of "parent" to my own mother, constantly calling to make sure she was taking care of herself and wasn't staying out too late. Mother, who always contended that she couldn't see well enough to drive at night, had suddenly become nocturnal!

Occasionally, I scolded her for running the roads with her girlfriends and staying on the phone continuously. She met her friends at five o'clock each morning to walk at the mall, and played dominoes or card games every night. On the rare occasions when I caught her at home by phone, she was so popular that we were constantly interrupted by her call-waiting.

I was thrilled when she announced she'd met and would soon be marrying a wonderfully sweet eighty-two-year-old man, Bill (whom I adore, by the way). What a relief! Maybe now she'd settle down and I'd have my mother back! It takes great courage to marry when you're sixteen, raise nine kids, bury two husbands, then fall hopelessly in love again and remarry when you're almost eighty! All that living, and people who meet my beautiful mom think she's only in her sixties.

More often than I acknowledge, I call upon Mama's legacy of faith, strength, humor, and zest for living. The eternal optimist, she taught me to look on the bright side of things, to make lemonade out of lemons, that every cloud has a silver lining, and to always smile and be kind to others. Simple truths, but wise axioms for living.

Since Mama is famous for saying, *"Give me my flowers while I'm living,"* it seemed only natural to throw Mama a surprise eightieth birthday party recently. When she walked into the reserved, flower-filled dining room, over seventy of her family and friends were anxiously waiting to hand her a fresh rose or a carnation.

At the end of a perfect day, my heart felt like it would burst as I watched my radiant mom dance with her children and sons-in-law to the song, "You Were Loved." Euphorically and blissfully content, I knew that for the legacy Mama had given, she'd received a fitting tribute to a life well lived.

We often take for granted those

wonderful attributes of our parents.

They not only enrich our lives but

they continue to live in us and in our

own children. Legacies are cherished

heirlooms of the heart.

Y ou are engraved on the palms of My hands. I am ever mindful of you and bless you. When you delight yourself in Me, I give you the very desires of your heart. Watch Me do far beyond all that you can ask or dream according to My power which is working in you. Taste and experience My goodness.

Bountiful Blessings,
Your 100% Faithful God

Isaiah 49:16; Psalm 115:12–13; Psalm 37:4;
Ephesians 3:20; Psalm 34:8

DINOSAUR DELIGHT

By LeAnn Weiss

*M*y sister Sharon is a talented mom and normally goes all out creating themed birthday parties for her two small boys. But as my nephew John's fourth birthday approached, Sharon was adjusting to a marital separation. To save money, Sharon decided to bake a homemade cake for John this year. Two days before John's birthday, Sharon and her boys were grocery shopping and walked by the bakery department. "Look, Mommy, that's the cake I want for my birthday! Let's get it now," John said, pointing to the green, dinosaur-shaped cake with a gleam in his eye.

Eyeing the price tag, Sharon's heart sank. Although the cake was under twenty dollars, it just wasn't in her budget. "Sweetheart, we'll have to wait because mommy doesn't have enough money," she said.

"Can't you use your credit card?" John proposed.

"Honey you have to pay for credit cards, too," Sharon explained, taking his small hand in hers. "But don't worry . . . God will take care of us," she enthusiastically added.

Later that day, I asked Sharon to deliver a package for me to my friend Billie, who runs My Father's Love food ministry. When Billie saw that Sharon's two children had come along, she said, "Wait right here."

Billie disappeared into the back room and came back minutes later holding something. "I thought your kids might enjoy this," Billie said, handing Sharon a clear plastic box containing a cake.

"Mommy, look . . . God gave me my birthday cake!" John exclaimed, pointing at the cake.

Tears ran from my sister's eyes as she looked at the cake that was identical in everything but color to the cake John had picked earlier that morning.

"Mommy, it's okay that it's yellow instead of green," John reassured my sister.

That cake was my sister's personal reminder that her Heavenly Father was watching over them. Sharon realized that if God cared enough to orchestrate something as special as a dinosaur cake to celebrate John's birthday, she could certainly trust him with their future.

God not only supplies all of our needs,

but sometimes he also surprises us by

blessing us with even our heart's

smallest desires.

*I*n this world, you'll face trouble. But you can take heart, knowing that I've already overcome the world. Don't let your heart be troubled or be afraid because I've given you My healing peace. Incline your heart to fear Me and keep all My commandments so that life may go well with your children and your children's children forever. Remember that all things are possible with Me!

My Everlasting Love,
Your Great Physician
and Promise Keeper

John 16:33; John 14:27; Deuteronomy 5:29; Mark 10:27

A HOUSE FULL OF HEARTS

By Caron Loveless

$\mathcal{F}$or forty-eight hours Joanne paced the hospital floor hoping for news that her daughter, Brianne, would survive. But the doctors made no promises. Her surgery had been extensive and all they could do was wait.

Countless times Brianne had been in the hospital for pneumonia and other illnesses related to a congenital heart defect. At three years old she weighed only twenty-five pounds, but her mother did her best to stay optimistic.

Still waiting word, and on the verge of exhaustion, Joanne drove home to the one-bedroom apartment she shared with Brianne. And when she got there something happened.

Everywhere she looked she saw hearts.

First, as she set her keys on the counter she noticed a greeting card from a concerned friend. There was a heart on the cover. Then, while reaching for the dish towel, she saw a heart appliqued in the middle of it. Later, she spied a long forgotten heart plaque on the wall and then, as she crashed into bed, right in front of her eyes flashed the hearts on Brianne's bedspread and her little heart outfit hanging in the closet.

All at once Joanne knew that her "heart sightings" were from God. It was as if he was trying to say, "I know you're anxious but do not be afraid. Your child is safely in my hands. Watch and see. I will make a way to heal her heart."

As Joanne sensed this, relief began to rush through her and, as her eyes filled with tears, all her anxiety rolled away. In its place fell a gentle, soothing peace. And when she woke from her nap she was amazed to find that a bright burst of hope was pulsing through her.

Brianne's surgery was a huge success. And the healing of her heart was the catalyst God used to ignite a fresh, abiding faith in Joanne. Today a heart theme abounds in every room of their home, giving glory to God and announcing to all that he is indeed the King of Hearts.

Trust your heart's condition to the steady hand of the

Great Physician. Show him the places that cause you

most pain. Let his powerful prescriptions cure all your

concerns and soothe your troubled soul with peace.

*T*imely words accomplish wonders and kind words refresh your child's anxious heart. Give your family members daily encouragement, building them up. Help them identify and get rid of the sin that so easily entangles them and anything else that holds them back from reaching My best for their lives. Cheer them on, helping them to run with endurance the unique course of life I've planned for each of them.

Purposely,
Your God of Hope

Proverbs 12:25; Proverbs 15:23; Hebrews 3:13; Hebrews 12:1

A MESSAGE FOR MIKEY

By Judy Carden

$\mathcal{M}$arianne's sixteen-year-old son's acts of disobedience had been coming in daily installments. Though she was annoyed with him, her heart prompted her to offer him direction, yet the words were hard to find. Instead, a familiar phrase she had relayed to him for years came to mind. So on a piece of blue-striped paper she wrote this message: "You are a gentleman and a scholar, and I shall dance at your wedding." She placed the note on his bed.

Marianne was lost in thought later that afternoon when Mikey popped his head into her bedroom doorway.

"Hey, Mom," he said. "I need to talk to you, but before I do, I want you to know that I was just feeling down—not suicidal or anything."

Rubbing the palms of his hands together, he continued, "After I got into trouble again last night, I sat in bed wondering whether, if I were gone, would it really make a difference? If I had died last year when I was real sick, would everybody be better off without me?"

Mikey let out a deep sigh, then continued, "Anyway, I figured maybe God forgot to give me a plan for my life because lately I'm a mess. So I asked him for a sign to let me know that he has a plan for my future. For that matter, that I even *have* a future. I wasn't asking him to appear in AP English class in golden robes, just for a little sign that would say, 'Hey, Mikey, I have a plan for your future.'"

Tears streaked Marianne's creamy complexion.

Mikey retrieved the blue-striped paper from the pocket of his varsity letter jacket and thrust it into her hand. "Just found this on my bed," he said, his husky voice quivering. "When I saw the note with the old saying that you will dance at my wedding, I knew it was God's little sign that I have a future after all."

Thank you, Lord, Marianne silently prayed, *for guiding my hands to write the very words you knew my Mikey needed to hear.*

Moms, never underestimate the

power of a few encouraging words.

They just might be the lifeline of

hope to your child's weary and

wounded heart.

$\mathcal{T}$ ake time to be still and know that I am God. Consider the great things I've done for you and your family. Impress My commandments on your children, talking about Me in your daily activities. Remember, My Word is useful for teaching, rebuking, correcting, and training your children in righteousness so that they may be thoroughly equipped for every good work.

Blessing You,

Your Always Faithful God

Psalm 46:10; 1 Samuel 12:24; Deuteronomy 6:6–7; 2 Timothy 3:16–17

BREAKFAST BLESSINGS

By LeAnn Weiss

$\mathcal{G}$rowing up, my family shared dinner around the table together each night. But for the most part, we were on our own for breakfast. Being a classic night owl, I'd sleep as late as I could and grab a bagel or an apple as I rushed out the door to catch my school bus.

But the school year Mom was pregnant, she made an extra effort each morning to make us hot breakfasts like oatmeal, scrambled eggs, or French toast. Mom wanted us to learn about the wonders of God and his daily involvement in the lives of his children. Starting in Exodus, she read the Bible to us for ten minutes each morning during breakfast. She created little interactive games, word pictures, and interesting dramas to accompany each of our short devotions.

One of our continuing games while we listened to Mom read was to spot as many good things as possible that God did for the Children of Israel. We talked about God's faithfulness in crisis situations, such as when he sent plagues to get his children out of Egypt or parted the Red Sea. But we also discussed God's little daily blessings, such as the manna he provided each day.

Another aspect of our game was identifying all the times God's people murmured and complained. Acting on God's instructions in his Word to remember the things he'd done, Mom helped us make a blessing basket. She gave us little strips of blank paper and asked us to write our names and something good God had done in our own lives. Then we folded the paper and put it in the basket. Frequently, we'd pull a strip from the basket and thank God.

When my baby sister Sarah was born, and the new school year began, we were back to breakfast on our own since Mom now had extra responsibilities. But those few minutes a day Mom invested imparting God's Word into our lives continue to feed my soul more than twenty years later. When I sometimes catch myself grumbling and complaining, God reminds me of Mom inspiring me to count his bountiful blessings.

As a mom, you play a major role in

shaping how your children view God.

Even in the routine of everyday life,

you can squeeze in moments to

nourish your children's souls, helping

them discover God's incomparable

character and blessings.

$\mathcal{L}$isten and come to Me. Hear Me that your soul may live! Experience My faithful love and covenant with you. When you put into practice what you learn and hear from Me, My perfect peace is with you and your family.

Peacefully,

Emanuel

_____   _____

Isaiah 55:3; Philippians 4:9

LISTEN TO THE MUSIC

By Caron Loveless

It was dinnertime, very close to Christmas, and there were packages to wrap and food to fix, but there was also music in the air.

It was harp music, on the stereo, and at first I didn't notice it, but the sound came so rich and pure that I paused in my work just to listen. That's when I felt the impression . . .

Why not stop and cherish this moment?

I tried to ignore it, but the thought came again, so, leaving lettuce in the sink, I dried my hands and walked to the room where my ten-year-old sat reading. There were no lights on, just the silvery beams of a rain-cast evening falling softly through the window. And the beauty of it caught me off guard. In that moment, my son seemed older and wiser, and I wondered where the time had gone. For a while I just stood there, looking at him and listening to the harps in the background.

"How's the book?" I asked as I kissed him.

"Good," he answered. "What are you looking at?"

"Just you, Honey."

"Oh," he said with a sheepish grin.

The younger ones were being far too quiet, but I found them out in the garage riding skateboards and making basketball hoops out of coat hangers . . . and, for once, playing happily together. I spied on them from a distance until the little one looked up and said, "Hi, Momma. You need something?"

"No, Sweetie. Just watching."

"Oh," he said, still riding in circles. "Watch me, Momma, watch me!"

"I see you, Honey . . . I see you . . . I do."

And for awhile I just stood there looking, just looking, in awe of my bonus of boys.

Of course, there was still dinner to fix and gifts to wrap, but there had also been some music in the air. Such a small thing, really, but I think God played it for me, hoping I would hear it and pause for just a while to revel in my children and to capture "Kodak moments" for the album of my heart.

Tune your ears to the sounds of God's

spirit as he prompts you to ponder

your life. Mark your most precious

moments. And rejoice in the gifts that

each day can bring, no matter what

season you're in.

*W*eeping lasts for a season, but in My time, I'll restore your joy. As high as the heavens are above the earth, so great is My incomparable love for you. From everlasting to everlasting, My love is with you and My righteousness with your children's children. I'll fill you with joy in My presence and eternal pleasures at My right hand.

Eternally,
Your Heavenly Father

Psalm 30:5; Psalm 103:11,17; Psalm 16:11

A CELEBRATION OF LOVE

By Susan Duke

$\mathcal{W}$hile driving to pick up the dozen balloons I'd ordered early that November morning, I found myself voicing a strange prayer request. "Lord, I know we're really not supposed to 'put out a fleece,' but sometimes I feel as if Thomas knows exactly what's going on down here! If there's a way for me to know that, could you give me some small sign?"

Six years had passed since I'd lost my son Thomas. Birthdays and holidays will always be fragile times, but after experiencing God's restoration and healing grace, I wanted to celebrate sweet memories on Thomas' birthday this year. I walked into the store, quickly sweeping thoughts of my prayer request from my mind. When the clerk handed me the colorful mass of balloons, she paused for a moment, walked a few steps over to another counter, and gathered another bundle. "I'm going to give you an extra dozen balloons today," she said. I made a mistake on another order and I just want you to have these. And I think I'll also throw in a giant silver *Happy Birthday* Mylar balloon! I do hope it's a birthday you're celebrating."

I simply said, "Thank you."

Well on my way to the cemetery, I heard a still small voice speak to my heart: *How many balloons do you have?*

Two dozen, I thought, *which is twenty-four . . . and the Mylar makes twenty-five.*

And how old is Thomas today?

"Twenty-five," I whispered.

Once at the cemetery, I gathered the balloons and walked to the spot where I let them go. Compared to the vastness of heaven, I felt small as I beheld the kaleidoscope of colors dancing upward into the buttermilk blue sky. Before releasing the last silver Mylar balloon, I hugged it tight and sent it to deliver my celebration of love to Thomas.

As the silver message faded from sight, I realized that, between heaven and hearts, there is no distance. Today I'd touched heaven and held its splendor in my hands. Celebrating life, both here and there, I envisioned Thomas standing with the Creator of all birthdays, smiling and waiting for twenty-five balloons to make their journey across heaven's gates.

The bond that exists between mother and child never

dies. God is faithful to remind us that love and life are

eternal and that heaven is as close

as a whispered prayer.

OTHER BOOKS BY STARBURST PUBLISHERS®

God Things Come in Small Packages: Celebrating the Little Things in Life
Susan Duke, LeAnn Weiss, Caron Loveless, and Judith Carden
God's generosity is limitless and His love can be revealed in many forms. From
a single bloom in winter to a chance meeting on a busy street, readers will be
encouraged to acknowledge God's generous hand in everyday life. Personalized
scripture is artfully combined with compelling stories and reflections.
(cloth) ISBN 1892016281 **$12.95**

God Things Come in Small Packages for Moms: Rejoicing in the Simple
Pleasures of Motherhood
Susan Duke, LeAnn Weiss, Caron Loveless, and Judith Carden
From life as a soccer mom to the first grandchild, most mothers spend their days
taking care of others. Now, busy moms will be reminded that God is taking care
of them through poignant stories recounting the everyday blessings of being a
mother. Each story combines personalized scripture with heartwarming
vignettes and inspiring reflections
(cloth) ISBN 189201629X **$12.95**

God's Abundance for Women: Devotions for a More Meaningful Life
Compiled by Kathy Collard Miller
Following the success of *God's Abundance*, this book will touch women of all ages
as they seek a more meaningful life. Essays from our most beloved Christian
authors exemplify how to gain the abundant life that Jesus promised through
trusting Him to fulfill our every need. Each story is enhanced with Scripture,
quotes, and practical tips providing brief, yet deeply spiritual reading.
(cloth) ISBN 1892016141 **$19.95**

Treasures of a Woman's Heart: A Daybook of Stories and Inspiration
Compiled by Lynn D. Morrissey
Join the best-selling editor of *Seasons of a Woman's Heart* in this touching sequel where she unlocks the treasures of women and glorifies God with scripture, reflection, and a compilation of stories. Explore heartfelt living with vignettes by Kay Arthur, Emilie Barnes, Claire Cloninger, and more
(cloth) 1-892016-25-7 **$18.95**

Purchasing Information
www.starburstpublishers.com

Books are available from your favorite bookstore, either from current stock or special order: use title, author, and ISBN. If unable to purchase from a bookstore, you may order direct from STARBURST PUBLISHERS. When ordering please enclose full payment plus shipping and handling as follows:

Post Office (4th class)
$3.00 with purchase of up to $20.00
$4.00 ($20.01–$50.00)
8% of purc hase price for purchases of $50.01 and up

Canada
$5.00 (up to $35.00)
15% ($35.01 and up)

United Parcel Service (UPS)
$4.50 (up to $20.00)
$6.00 ($20.01–$50.00)
12% ($50.01 and up)

Overseas
$5.00 (up to $25.00)
20% ($25.01 and up)

Payment in U.S. funds only. Please allow two to three weeks minimum (longer overseas) for delivery. Make checks payable to and mail to: Starburst Publishers®, P.O. Box 4123, Lancaster, PA 17604. Credit card orders may be placed by calling 1-800-441-1456, Mon–Fri, 8:30 A.M. to 5:30 P.M. Eastern Standard Time. Prices are subject to change without notice. Catalogs are available for a 9 x 12 self-addressed envelope with four first-class stamps.